3/18

OUTDOOR EXPLORERS

Northeast

3

Helen Foster James

Published in the United States of America
by Cherry Lake Publishing
Ann Arbor, Michigan
www.cherrylakepublishing.com

Reading Adviser: Marla Conn MS, Ed., Literacy specialist, Read-Ability, Inc.

Photo Credits: © Monkey Business Images / Shutterstock.com, cover, 1;
© NadyaEugene / Shutterstock.com, 6; © Olga Ustynova / Shutterstock.com,
8, 12; © CatbirdHill / Shutterstock.com, 10; © SNEHIT / Shutterstock.com, 10;
© Jason Patrick Ross / Shutterstock.com, 11; © Georgy Markov / Shutterstock.
com, 11; © Sarah Jessup / Shutterstock.com, 12; © ClubhouseArts /
Shutterstock.com , 13; © Imladris / Shutterstock.com, 13; © FotoRequest /
Shutterstock.com, 14, 17; © RRuntsch / Shutterstock.com, 16; © BMJ /
Shutterstock.com, 16; © winuturn / Shutterstock.com, 17; © BufferedBrain /
Shutterstock.com, 18; © JFunk / Shutterstock.com, 18; © Jay Ondreicka /
Shutterstock.com, 19; © Jim Cumming / Shutterstock.com, 19; © Efimenko
Alexander / Shutterstock.com, 20; © Dmitry Naumov / Shutterstock.com, 20;
© SP-Photo / Shutterstock.com, 20; © XiXinXing / Shutterstock.com, 20;
© K Steve Cope / Shutterstock.com, 22; © Eric Urquhart / Shutterstock.com,
22; © jpreat / Shutterstock.com, 22; © Dan Schreiber / Shutterstock.com, 22

Library of Congress Cataloging-in-Publication Data
Names: James, Helen Foster, 1951- author.
Title: Northeast / Helen Foster James.
Description: Ann Arbor : Cherry Lake Publishing, 2017. | Series: Outdoor
    explorers | Includes bibliographical references and index. | Audience:
    Grades K to 3.
Identifiers: LCCN 2016057046| ISBN 9781634728744 (hardcover) | ISBN
    9781634729635 (pdf) | ISBN 9781534100527 (pbk.) | ISBN 9781534101418
    (hosted ebook)
Subjects: LCSH: Natural history—Northeastern States—Juvenile literature.
Classification: LCC QH104.5.N58 J36 2017 | DDC 508.74—dc23
LC record available at https://lccn.loc.gov/2016057046

Cherry Lake Publishing would like to acknowledge the work of the Partnership
for 21st Century Skills. Please visit www.p21.org for more information.

Printed in the United States of America
Corporate Graphics

Table of Contents

SOTA

WISCONSIN

MICHIGAN

IOWA

NEW YORK

MAINE

VERMONT

NEW HAMPSHIRE

MASSACHUSETTS

PENNSYLVANIA

RHODE ISLAND

CONNECTICUT

ILLINOIS INDIANA OHIO

NEW JERSEY

DELAWARE

WEST
VIRGINIA

MARYLAND

MISSOURI

KENTUCKY

VIRGINIA

TENNESSEE

NORTH
CAROLINA

ARKANSAS

SOUTH
CAROLINA

ALABAMA GEORGIA

MISSISSIPPI

LOUISIANA

FLORIDA

	Midwest
	Northeast
	Southeast
	Southwest
	West

Northeast Facts

Average winter: 27°F (-2.7°C)

Average summer: 68.6°F (20.3°C)

Lowest point: Sea level

Highest point: 6,288 feet (1,916.5 m) Mount
Washington, New Hampshire

Smallest state: Rhode Island
- 1,212 square miles (3,139 sq km)
- 33% water
- 66.9% land

Largest state: New York
- 54,554 square miles (141,294 sq km)
- 13.6% water
- 86.3% land

It's time for a nature hike.
Let's see what we can see.

New Hampshire's official state flower, the purple lilac, is able to survive severe winters. How do you think this happens?

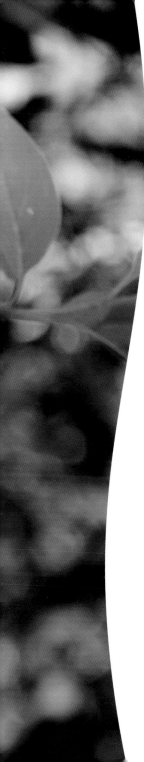

Plants

Some flowers are small. They are hard to find. I look for purple lilacs. They grow tall. They are easy to find.

Look at the maple trees. Their leaves change color in the fall. It's fun to collect the fallen leaves. They're red, orange, yellow, and brown.

American Holly Tree

- Delaware's official state tree since 1939.

- The ends of the leaves are sharp and the berries are poisonous.

Black-eyed Susan

- Maryland's official state flower since 1918.

- This wildflower has been used as medicine for centuries.

Eastern Hemlock Tree

- Pennsylvania's official state tree since 1931.

- These trees can live over 800 years.

Eastern White Pine Tree

- Maine's official state tree since 1945.

- This fast-growing tree can grow over 24 inches (60.9 centimeters) in a year.

Mayflower

- Massachusetts' official state flower since 1918.

- These tiny flowers grow low to the ground.

Purple Lilac

- These flowers can be found in parks and forests.

- They can grow as tall as 10 feet (3 meters) and live for over 100 years.

Sugar Maple Tree

- Official state tree of Vermont and New York.

- Maple seeds look like helicopters when they fall from the tree.

Violet

- Official state flower of New Jersey and Rhode Island.

- The petals can be used in desserts, like cakes and cookies.

Maine and Massachusetts' official state
bird is the black-capped chickadee.
Why do you think the bird is named this?

Animals

I look. I watch a squirrel climb up a tree. Is it looking for food?

I listen. I hear a chickadee. It sings chick-a-dee-dee-dee.

I see a flash of brown and white between the trees.
Do I see a deer and her fawn?

American Robin

- Connecticut's official state bird since 1943.

- Only the male robin sings.

Beaver

- New York's official state mammal since 1975.

- Their front teeth never stop growing.

Black-capped Chickadee

- These songbirds can be found in forests, parks, and fields.

- They hide their food, like seeds, to eat later.

Eastern Gray Squirrel

- A common squirrel found in the Northeast.

- They eat almost everything, sometimes even frogs and small birds.

Garter Snake

- Massachusetts' official state reptile since 2007.

- These harmless snakes hibernate during winter.

Mallard Duck

- This common duck can be found near lakes, ponds, and rivers.

- Ducklings, or baby ducks, can swim the same day they hatch.

Red-spotted Newt

- New Hampshire's official state amphibian since 1985.

- They can be found near slow-moving water, like ponds.

White-tailed Deer

- Official state animal of New Hampshire and Pennsylvania.

- Fawns, or baby deer, are born with white spots.

Spring

Summer

Fall

Winter

Weather

The spring air is still cool. Sometimes it's foggy.

The sun is out longer in the summer. The ground feels warm.

I watch the leaves change color in the fall. The wind blows the leaves off the trees. I kick them as I walk.

The winter is cold. Sometimes I catch snowflakes on my tongue.

Forest

Lake

Meadow

Mountain

Geography

I **wander** into a forest. It looks dark. The trees are blocking out the sun.

I walk by a lake. There are many trees growing by it.

I pass through a **meadow** in the mountains. Butterflies are on some flowers.

Where would you like to hike?

Find Out More

Ehlert, Lois. *Red Leaf, Yellow Leaf.* San Diego: Harcourt Brace Jovanovich, 1991.

Louv, Richard. *Last Child in the Woods: Saving Our Children from Nature-Deficit Disorder.* Chapel Hill: Algonquin Books, 2008.

Glossary

amphibian (am-FIB-ee-uhn) a cold-blooded animal that lives in water and breathes with gills when young; as an adult, it develops lungs and lives on land

hibernate (HYE-bur-nate) to sleep or be inactive during winter

mammal (MAM-uhl) a warm-blooded animal that has hair or fur and usually gives birth to live babies; female mammals produce milk to feed their young

meadow (MED-oh) a grassy field, sometimes used for grazing or for growing hay

medicine (MED-ih-sin) helpful drugs used to treat illnesses

poisonous (POI-zuh-nuhs) having a poison that can harm or kill

reptile (REP-tile) a cold-blooded animal with scaly, dry skin that crawls across the ground or creeps on short legs

wander (WAHN-dur) to walk around without a particular purpose

Index

About the Author

Helen Foster James is a volunteer interpretive naturalist for her local state park. She lives by the ocean and loves to hike in the mountains. She is the author of *S Is for S'mores: A Camping Alphabet* and more than 20 other books for children.